Aftermath

Aftermath

JILL YAMASAWA

Kahuaomānoa Press
Honolulu, Hawai‘i

-Kahuaomānoa Press-

President & Chief Editor	Brandy Nālani McDougall
Vice-President & Managing Editor	Ann Inoshita
Associate Editor & Treasurer	Ryan Oishi
Assistant Editors	Kai Gaspar,
	Chelsey Kojima,
	Bryan Kamaoli Kuwada,
	Christina Low,
	Anjoli Roy,
	Aiko Yamashiro
Faculty Advisor	Robert Sullivan
Typesetting & Book Design	Brent Fujinaka

Cover image by Ryuta Nakajima.

"B(u)y a Handkerchief" was previously published in *How2*. Versions of "Pennies for Calvin," "Star Wars" (now titled "Who I Know"), "A Long Walk of Thresholds," "Out of Mānoa," "Sedilia," "Lawa," "Referral 4," "Catchment," "What We Get," "Real Lives," and "Homeland Security" were published in *Tinfish 18 1/2: The Book*.

Kahuaomānoa means, in ʻōlelo Hawaiʻi, "the fruit of Mānoa" and "foundation of Mānoa."

Kahuaomānoa Press is dedicated toward the publication and promotion of excellence in student art and literature. As such, every effort is made to privilege the student voice and perspective first and foremost.

Acknowledgements

Love and gratitude to my mother, father, brother, Grandma Jean, Honaunau grandparents, aunties, uncles, cousins, and friends especially Aunty Carol Rogers of the Kona Arts Center, Aunty Mary Wataru, Erika Kunimura and Aunty Penny Fujita. Mahalo to Susan M. Schultz, my professor and mentor. Props to professors of Santa Clara University and University of Hawaiʻi at Mānoa, in particular Eileen Ragazzi Elrod, Ryuta Nakajima, John Zuern, Scott Garson, and Jonathan P. Hunt. I'm indebted to public school educators like Keri Debusca at McKinley, Ellen Schroeder at Olomana and my elementary teachers at Holualoa El like Susan Finley. Thanks to the students who named me Shirley. My appreciation to the staff of Kahuaomānoa Press for editing. To my fellow poets, Tiare, Santigie, Kai, and Brandy, thanks for writing so others may read. I am humbled by the Pacific Ocean and all that sustains and connects.

Contents

Equations

Foreword

In 2007, Jill Yamasawa transcribed the voices of her McKinley High School students, edited them, lasered the poems onto fine paper, sewed the chapbooks together. She called the collection *Seeds & Esssse* and presented copies to the students who had given their words to her. It is a beautiful book in so many ways. Many of these students live in Mayor Wright Housing; their poems are not odes to joy, but sterner stuff. One writes, "Lots of people wants to see what's my mind's like. There's no colors in my head, but black and white." Another: "Crying is like the color of a white wave hitting the sand. / It tastes like cotton candy at a carnival . . . / Crying is dangerous." And another: "It kinda hurt when you alone like me." Aftermath is a sequel to that small, but significant book. It is the biography of a place, McKinley High School. It is a gift to us from someone who, as teacher and as writer, listens and listens profoundly, to the voices around her. They speak of struggle and loss—not losses about which we can easily feel nostalgic, but searing ones. Cultures, languages, families, jobs, lives lost.

And words lost. Like so many places in Hawai'i, McKinley High School is only the most recent building, name, ideological construct for what have been other names, other uses, other cultural values. The problem of memory is inscribed in the names used to mark places in Hawai'i. To the winner go the names. What is now called Ford Island (at Pearl Harbor) was Moku'ume'ume, Chinaman's Hat was Mokoli'i, Diamond Head was Leahi, and so on. McKinley High School was built in Kewalo. Or consider the name "Pele." In "Madame Pele," Yamasawa offers up the many meanings of the words "Madame" and "Pele," moving as far afield as the Brazilian soccer player, Pele. In Hawai'i many know Pele as the volcano goddess, a spiritual life force. But the astounding turn in Yamasawa's poem comes here:

> I mean the bomber so named before its presentation
> to the Air Force by McKinley High School students after
> a successful bond drive to cover the cost.

This would be during the Second World War, Pele's name appropriated by the military for a very different kind of firepower. Yamasawa draws attention to other words, as well, from "Homeland Security," "Mission Accomplished," and many others. She writes in standard English, Pidgin, and in Hawaiian words the historical record had suppressed.

Yamasawa builds her project on an axis. On the synchronic line is the study of mathematics; Yamasawa's narrator, Shirley, is a special ed math teacher at McKinley High School. The other, diachronic line represents history. This is where logic and sense threaten at every turn to collapse, whether because a student has no family to record on his family tree project, or because McKinley High School itself is a colonial implant on the ʻāina. While the sections of her book are titled with the reassuring words, "slope," "variables," "equations," and where even "inequalities" takes on a neutral cast, what falls into these categories is less easily organized. While Shirley can teach math, it is clear that most of what is to be learned (via Shirley) is about Hawaiʻi's social and economic inequalities, its fraught linguistic history, its various amnesias (including those of the present about the present). There are moments in the text where these axes come together violently, as in "A Long Walk of Thresholds":

> There's an Original Sin
> that taints our country. The radicals wrote
> men and women are created equal.

The historical radicals—before McKinley—set down an ideal line that could not bear the weight of American history.

Jill Yamasawa's documentary poetry reflects the poet's own capacity to empathize with her students, caught up in domestic dramas that are also national in scope. Nowhere in the book are we permitted to forget the Iraq War or the military recruiters who have settled just off-campus. Yamasawa has given us the words, the voices, and some of the images. If we are to act ethically, we must look and listen.

Susan M. Schultz
February 7, 2009

To my mother, my teacher
and my father, my Will

The 1933 McKinley High School Band marches in formation. At one time there was a girls fife and drum corps. In the 1910s McKinley had a small orchestra.

Find the Slope

During the war, servicemen visited McKinley's campus. They were impressed by the enthusiastic response of students in the sale of U.S. savings bonds and stamps.

We need

Hawaii

just as much and
a good deal
more

than we did
California.

It

is Manifest Destiny.

President William McKinley

Kewalo[1]

A fishpond and surrounding land
on the plains below King Street,
and beyond Koula. It contains
a spring rather famous in the times
previous to the conversion to Christianity,
as the place where victims
designed for the Heiau of Kanelaau on Punchbowl slopes,
first drowned. The priest when holding
the victim's head under
water would say to her or him
on any signs of struggling,
"Moe malie i ke kai o ko haku."
"Lie still in the waters of your superior."
From this it was called Kawailumalumai,
"Drowning waters."

Dictionary of Hawaiian Localities
Saturday Press, Oct. 6, 1883

Servicemen PFC L.L. Mitchell and PFC Julius J. Stedtal observe the work of the Black and Gold Staff. On May Day, 1942, five hundred service men visited the McKinley campus and were presented with leis.

Where I Am

Pregnant clouds delivered rain
for forty-three days, then left.

Some considered it a cleansing,
a purification for past sins.

To American viewers,
it was a biblical downpour[2],
bullets piercing the island,
punishment by flood.

Still others felt the rain's desperation,
its desire to reclaim
the marshlands. But

the land was not fulfilled.
I fear it was not first nor
primed to receive the water.

Foreword: McKinley High, A Public School[3]

McKinley High School has contributed mightily
to the growth of *this* community.
Its alumni have poured into
the mainstream of American life
in times of peace and stress.
McKinley points with just pride
to the accomplishments of its illustrious graduates
in the fields of politics,
engineering, science, medicine,
law, education, government
service, business, the fine arts and
entertainment. Many have carried
the word of God to the people.

The school is forging
ahead in art, music, mathematics,
dramatics, publications, science,
English, foreign languages, history,
and ROTC. A look through these pages
should inspire the reader
with the dynamic movement within
a modern public high school.

Yet, by far the greatest contribution
McKinley HS has made and will
continue to make is its masses
of graduates, nameless

in many instances, who serve
their respective communities
in the entire gamut
of honest human endeavor.

The day-to-day average citizen
who produces
goods and services,

who strives to provide
the best for his family
by the sweat of his brow,
who respects
law and order,
and who furnishes
the sinews of war
in times of international conflict,
is McKinley's claim to greatness.

Like Cornelia, mother of Roman Gracchi,
McKinley echoes:
"These are my jewels.
I give them
to my country."

Teichiro Hirata
        Principal

*Students of Mrs. Faulconer's Health and
Safety class are given drills to increase
their speed in putting on their gas masks.*

Sedilia

Do you know the alma mater[4]
still plays the lyric of the dead?
"Loyal serve" severs
the melody. You see smiling
faces, stoic faces, when you march
down this hall.

Here we get plenny fighter jets and
helicopters. We get plenny red
shirts, red shoes, dyed hair,
bolo heads, MWH & WELA tattoos,
Piru Boyz 4 Life graffiti,
and JROTC uniforms.

From a Chinatown church basement
to Princess Ruth's castle
to other locations of insurance claim importance
to this place of sea, of marsh, of wetl&.
My last name, Yamasawa,
山沢, mountain stream, mountain marsh.
Sawa, 沢, small stream, small marsh,
from Hiroshima to Kewalo only to meet up
with an emptied stream,
an emptied marsh.

The heat comm&s us outside
under the giant canopies, our bunkers.
We are blind to all color except
the black & gold for Princeton[5],
for the Monarchy.
McKinley in the center,
flagpole in the center,
& us on the side like Korean Sushi,
like the JROTC.
"Did you know Lost
shot McKinley in the back
-ground[6]? What would Reverend
Maurice Beckwith think

if he saw us now'?
A half Buddhist teaching Christian children
how to order radicals &
inequalities on a number line?

My students pile on one another,
their arms & legs a heap of limbs.
At a distance, if you didn't know
them, they'd seem to such an observer,
only a collection
of bodies.

J, who's 6'4, 240, jumps on top.
There's a collective moan.
For a moment, I panic;
they don't have
the proper equipment:
no helmets,
no pads,
no protection, but
I allow them to play on.
They love it,
& it's only one day until the end
of school.

The ground feels shriveled
as if ready to become a desert.
We are drowning
in this terrible heat.
The students are restless for a change
of temperature. K moans,
"This is hell.
I want waterrr!
Can I please have waterrr?"

It's hot, *puff out the hot-air balloon now,*
it is about to burst, it is bursting
with something invisible.

S is at the bottom, holding
on to the football.
The pile grows larger,
but he won't let go.
It's what he's been taught;
it's what I've taught him,
I'm ashamed to say.

We mimic the leaves of a tree,
turn to the sun;
our veins full of Tang & Shasta from
Times & Safeway. This conversation
is like a freed tiger
only to end recaptured or dead.

To be a Vienna sausage,
I keep pulling out your teeth,
believing a new set will appear
(it's what I've been told)
& I think at some point
you'd like to know why.

Behind McKinley & to the left is
the U.S. Army Recruiting Center.
To the left, to the left, everything you own
in a box to the left.
'Cause the truth of the matter
is replacing you is so easy.

Repeat.

Behind McKinley & to the left is
the U.S. Marine Recruiting Center.
To the left, to the left, everything you own
in a box to the left.
'Cause the truth of the matter
is replacing you is so easy.

Repeat.

S yells, "McKinley was a racist,"
and pretends to aim the football for his head.

We are not on a conveyor belt.
There are too many words
like *onomatopoeia* & *chee-hoo.*
Like *esoteric* & *Tokelauan.*
It took me nine months
to find the Times they meant,
no, the one on Vineyard;
to memorize W liked seed,
A didn't eat chocolate,
B ate strawberries only when paired with sugar & Cool Whip,
K just like suck on lemons, &
J didn't care—he would eat anything.

The Ward Estate's groundskeeper chased
kolohe students exiting school through the broken
fence. His name shoots
in & out of my memory like a Blue Angel.
"Get outta hea you kids."
I imagine his voice, deep & calm
as open water.
We hear, & sometimes learn,
pressing so close. A foreign vessel
off the coast, inhabiting the reef
like evil in live, written in inequalities:
Kukui Gardens>Lanakila>MWH.
During lunch when a student
came to the locked
door, sobbing, Mrs. H turned him away.
"I don't allow students inside
during my free time."
She turned to me a moment later & said:
"The tall boy, the giant,
I forget his name,
he wanted to talk to you.

But I sent him away
cause I need
my peace."
Peace be with you.
And Peace be with you.
She didn't underst& then
& maybe I don't underst& either.

With the grit
of chocolate milk on
our tongues,
we savor
the last bit of watery poi.
It's not enough,
but it has to be

History Tests

Many tests. Not of wills.
But some of that too.
They disappear in the sky
between Kaua'i and O'ahu, exploding
missiles, only to reappear
as infrared images
on the six o'clock news.

Test 1
Fill in the _____.
I told S I saw Min in the health room.
His friend asks, "Min?"
S answers, "Min Joong."

Test 2
Silent Reading.
In Viet Nam, leaflets fell from planes,
instructions in a foreign language
explaining evacuation.
The next day
the bombs came.

Test 3
Matching.
S places the letter "G"
next to question number one: territories.
G. *a person filled with single-minded zeal,*
esp. for an extreme religious or political cause.
C should have placed "G"
next to number two: fanatic.

Test 4
Vocabulary.
S tells me his name is gone,
already changed by the newspaper.
He sees things that aren't there.
He writes: Some girls are <u>fantastic</u>,
inserts a "t" and an "s" where they never existed.
He writes, "There are too many <u>stars</u>
on the <u>flag</u>."

B(u)y a Handkerchief

The following places were either annexed, put under treaty, or became territories during the reign of President McKinley or these places have high schools, statues, libraries, or other buildings in his honor.

PI
Hawai'i
Guam
Puerto Rico
Cuba

Arcata
Redlands
Bakersfield
McKinleyville

The 500
T Street, DC
Philadelphia
Walden
Fort Hamilton
Buffalo

Meadville
Scranton
Antietam Battlefield
Fort Gratiot
Port Huron

Dayton
Canton
Toledo
Lakewood
Sebring
Niles

St. Louis
Arlington
Beaverton
Casper, Wyoming

Mayaguez
Honolulu (((February 23, 1911[8])))
McKinley C, New Mexico
Mt. McKinley, Alaska

May you never be concealed
by a handkerchief[9],
but if (((when))) you are, buy a handkerchief.

A Long Walk of Thresholds[10]

"I saw an <u>immigrant</u> yesterday,"
S writes in his word bank.
Frederick Douglass is asked to speak
at a Fourth of July celebration.
On YouTube, Danny Glover reads
the speech, his voice quivers:
"Bombast! Fraud! Impiety!"
"The <u>overseer</u> did not know
he was a slave."

"The floor is filthy!"
"So get a mop and bucket."
"The <u>labor union</u> was killed
by a volcano."
"I'm tired of discussions.
Let's *do* something."
Walter Hunt invented
the safety pin and the sewing machine.
Ultimately, he did not pursue
its production, he worried
seamstresses would lose their jobs.
"I took all my weapons
and <u>assimilated</u> to China."

Kate Chopin sits on my desk.
I determine which words belong in vocabulary.
Peggy McIntosh sits on my desk.
I decide to trash her. Maybe not.
Retrieve her from trash.
Barack Obama sits on my desk, stapled.
Where's Kenya? "In Canada!"
Where's Kansas? "In Kentucky!"

Eileen Elrod sits on my desk with *piety and dissent.*
Maybe we're still sitting there, holding the Bible,
but not doing the hard work.
I mean this isn't Bleeding Kansas. Just a human Wright.
Not anything cruel or unusual.

"Things are better now. There is no slavery."
In this country. Between races.
Only between sexes. Crawls the sly predator.

There's an Original Sin
that taints our country. The radicals wrote
men and women are created equal.
Remember Mary Chestnut's diary.
How did she define "decent?"
Is it what we now call *their* culture?
Remember the big cane Preston Brooke used to hit
Charles Sumner? He did not intend to kill
Sumner, if he had, Brooke said he would have
used a different weapon.

"My strategy is to have a strategy."
What's so supreme about a taco? About a court?
Ask Roger Taney how law is decided.
Like Douglass predicted, we all wear cotton clothes.
The Truth is not a relative of mine,
but I think of her words, those weevils;
they're still in the Constitution.
"The Nativist was an immigrant
and she wore a green hat."

"The rebel ate a cheeseburger."
"We're in constant revision.
When you become a citizen,
there are two tables as you walk out
of the building, one
to register you as a democrat,
the other for a republican."
Lincoln didn't win
the majority of the popular vote.
When he ran for president
there were four candidates.
"Knock, knock." "Who's there?"
"Martial Law."

20

At Kakaako[11]

Kakaako was once a thriving community
with agricultural terraces,
residences of aliʻi[12],
and docks for foreign ships.

Kamehameha I had a residence,
along with his family, and personal kahuna.

Kakaako, also known as Kewalo,
according to archaeological *reports,*
was a place of recreation,
particularly around the shoreline.

The waters were used for cleansing,
fishing, canoe landings, and religious practices.

All Things, Beings, Equals[13]

Streams are complex
dynamic systems,
ever-changing in response
to external factors,
be it precipitation,
a landslide, or
man's intervention.

Every stream is always
striving for an equilibrium state, which
it never quite reaches, at least
not along its entire length,
and never anywhere for very long.

Image from *Victoria Ward and Her Family:
Memories of the Old Plantation*

A white fence
unbroken
2 (or 3) visible ponds
kiawe(?) trees
man-made stream(?)
no aqueducts just
a duck house(?) in
marshlands and part
of a coconut tree, in the distance
                              to the left
                              to the left
is a grove of them;
everything you own
in *a* marsh / march *to the left.*

then water
water
water and land
            water
            land and water
            water and land
                        water;
apparitions,
Leahi in the clouds

What We Get[14]

born and raised
in Kona, Hawai'i;
work and live
in Kona, O'ahu

in Kona
we get paulz place
doris place
post office
Hulihe'e palace
tako bell
pizza hut
macys
kmart
walmart
dennys
borders
starbucks
wendys
burger king
killer tacos
scottys aquarium
scottys video
kta
food 4 less where you gotta bag your own groceries
american savings
bank of Hawaii
first Hawaiian bank
central Pacific bank
federal credit union
Pu'uhonua o Honaunau
Queens bath
Kiholo
Puako
Makalapua
Kua bay
plenny construction jobs
traffic

small roads
cars
2 little rain
2 movie theaters
Aliʻi drive where all the tourists go
1 public pool by baby pond
5 baseball fields at old a's
2 high schools
plenny fancy hotels, cant name um all
4 no 5 private schools
2 mcdonalds
and 1 hospital
thats all the stuff Kona get

we get plenny stuff
but we get little bit stuff
you know what i mean

i not saying Kona
is betta than Kona
i just listing the stuff Kona get

S, on Perrier

S walks up to Mrs. H's desk
and points to her bottle of Perrier.
"You shouldn't drink that," he says.
She doesn't respond.
"I saw it on *Oprah*," he continues,
"there's something in it.
It's bad for you.
You could die."
Mrs. H stops her work.
"Young man," she says, "I don't know who you are.
Please get away
from my desk."

Mrs. H looks at me,
"Isn't he one of yours?"
"S, please come back over here," I say.
"But fo real," he turns to me,
"I'm not lying Miss Shirley.
I saw it this morning on the news.
Don't let her drink that."

S comes to my desk. "Have I ever lied to you?" he asks.
"I'm telling you, Miss, the green water,
it's got something bad in it.
Don't let her drink it. I promise.
Don't google it.
I wouldn't lie to you.
I swear. It's poisoned."

Inequalities

Major General Robert L. Stevenson

You, always in the act of leaving. Left. Left. Left. *Right.* Left.

The letters you wrote hang on
my wall, large and proud like
the letters at graduation.

Madame Pele

Do you know of Madame Pele?

Not Madame as in the title or form
of address to a French-speaking woman,
nor the English connotation of respect,
nor as in the head of a brothel, or
a "title for women in artistic or exotic
occupations, such as musicians or fortune-tellers."

Do you know of Madame Pele?

Not Pele as in the akua
many Kanaka Maoli trace their genealogy,
nor the famous footballer from Brazil;
nor the variant spelling of "peel" from Old French,
meaning "to remove the skin
from a fruit, vegetable, or shrimp";
not from the base "pangere, to fix, plant";
not like the baker's tool used "to carry
loaves of bread and pies out of an oven";
not da gurl dat wen grad Konawaena couple yeeahs aheada me;
and definitely not like the "small square defensive
tower, of the kind built in the 16th century
in the border counties of England and Scotland."

I mean the bomber plane so named before its presentation
to the Air Force by McKinley High School students after
a successful bond drive to cover the cost.

Homeland Security

Dad says we need to have a *real* address.
Before the State can issue us a street name,
my father names the narrow dirt passage,
Hikiwale Street and mails it off.

J, who's a junior, comes to visit me
during lunch. He says his brother just got stationed
in Alaska so his mom told him he has to move
there cuz he's almost too old for her
since he's nearly 18.
What's your brother doing in Alaska? I ask.
J wipes his cheeks, "Guarding the coast."

Vocabulary

It's the first day of school. *Verify.* It's the English vocab word of the day. Mrs. H points to another word: *Kokua.* It's the Hawaiian vocab word of the day. She points to it as the students enter the room. When everyone is settled, she begins to ask for nicknames. A student tells Mrs. H his Hawaiian name. She looks at her attendance sheet checking his last name, "Are you Hawaiian?" "Yes," he says, "my mom is 37.5%." She pauses. "Really? Well, how did you get your name?" He half shrugs, "My dad knew what it was from before, but he went to the ABC store to verify." Mrs. H smiles, "Wonderful," she says, "I'm so glad that you were able to use today's vocab word."

The Handbook

Maintain order,
obtain the standards,
target the benchmarks,
input in ECSSS by timeline,
drill in the GLOs.

School Security

T is nearly done with his work when
the retired cop, our security guard, Mr. X,
strides in and marches straight to T.

At first, Mr. X is calm and then he begins
to yell. T says nothing. Mr. X threatens
to call his mother and have her come in.
T shrugs, "She doesn't speak English."
Mr. X yells that he will have T suspended.
T says he doesn't care.

Mr. X's face turns red and he starts claiming
T will fail in school, in life.
T looks at me, "Are you gonna fail me?"
Mr. X growls, "Don't fall for his innocent act."
He retreats, taking T with him.

My students do not look up from their work,
but they are all listening for my voice,
waiting for me to signal
it is O.K. to speak.

"What was that about?" I ask.
J answers, "That thing that happened
yesterday with those people
in the oval by the statute."

Who I Know

I don't know many people in the service.
I only know a former student, Damien,
who enlisted the day after graduation.
Just Alan who's in the navy.
And Colin somewhere off the coast of California.
And Akira serving in New York and
Mitoshi who graduated from West Point.
And just Cassie's husband, Lopaka,
who was stationed in Kāneʻohe and
is now working off the coast of Japan.
His next tour may be off the coast of Iraq.
Yesterday he fell asleep
at the baby shower.
Just my former boyfriend, Jon,
who went to Saudi Arabia.
When I wrote him
an email to ask how he was,
his girlfriend responded: *Do not ever ever*
contact Jon again. He cannot be trusted.
And Jorge, my cousin's father, sent to Iraq.
And my great uncle, Toshio,
who was a part of the 442nd
and the 100th battalion.

And then there's just my grandfather,
"Uncle Tony," who volunteered for WWII.
He was a part of the "Old Boy" network,
a Kauaʻi mayor, and planned the freeway system
we have today—a freeway system, which has failed.
He passed on very little to my mother. Only asthma.

Her nebulizer, her IV bags, soldiers
fighting to keep her safe,
free to breath. Tissues like landmines
around her body. Another tour
of the Kona Hospital's meager facilities.
The wheezing, the coughing fits.
Nothing would secure
her lungs. Gasping for air
became a part of life.

War poster contest sponsored by Junior Civilian Defense Corps and the High School Victory Corps. Alberta Ogen, third grade, Kapalama School, poses with the winning posters of Melvin Liqua, third grade, Likelike School, and Ernest Morimoto, senior, McKinley High School.

(image copy*right*ed: unable to display)

young girl holds 2 posters
the first poster on the left (higher)
smiling
in plaid
dress
smart
shoes
background
gray wall, cement
or something similar

Poster 1 reads: KEEP
　　　　　　　'EM
　　　　　　　　BUYING
(image) a silver missile
　　　　smoke
　　　　fire
　　　　2 shadows
　　　　　　　　　BONDS
FOR

BOMBS

HIGH SCHOOL VICTORY CORPS

Poster 2 reads: **DONALD SAYS**

(image) Donald Duck
　　　　in sailor uniform

　　**"BUY BONDS
　　DON'T DUCK
　　YOUR DUTY"**

Mendied

Shineyourshoes, boy. Shine them good.
No tattoosorhearts (below the elbow),
where you're headedmaymirrorSomalia
andKosovo. It's been a draining day.
Pleasetellmetherifleis a paint gun.
Iwillthinkof you when Ipurchase M&Ms.

"[Boy-] [m]en die that others may live
in a better world." Moreletterswon't
fit;they'resmashed.

A mongoose destroying
two snakes' eggs.

We sit apart,
a part, of T H I S,
trying to grasp
a past shoe, but it flutters
away, past to the banyans
with the little yellow
bugs that only come
out during commencement.

The McKinley Color Guard, 1928

Pennies for Calvin

I took out a pen and wrote your name.
I made four copies and sent one
to the police. All the spines you broke
are still on the floor.
They won't take you with terroristic threatening
on your record. You came in yelling,
then crying saying, your future's gone;
you might as well die now.

I think back to the farm,
the grooves in earth from the roots
of the trees. I learned each curve
where the water cut into the soft dirt,
creating ravines and bogs,
miniature water systems
as intricate as the Tigris.
Mend the rock wall.
Pick the cherry.
Spray the poison.
I see cities on these walls.
Towns of hollow tile.
Each rectangle bound by four roads.

We watched the principal of
Kalihi Uka deploy to Iraq.
We sent pennies
for his 322nd Brigade.
We wrote letters saying,
"We'll miss you" and "Be safe."

Variables

Brigadier General Francis Takemoto, Hawaii National Guard, helps with plans for the May 14 Centennial Memorial Services in honor of the Hawai'i war dead.

What Kewalo Means to Me
to Me
By _____

this outcry
near mouths
empties
(into) you

In the end (((beginning and middle)))   (((you))) rise

          from the sea
          where
          the (((marsh and stream)))

                                                   appear

                                                   to have lost

                                                                      (((there
there; their)))
                                                   ¡dentities.[15]

Critical federal report opens
high school education to all[16]

McKinley HS, always been one nonstandard schoo

Unlike English Standard schools that had strict admission policies to keep the "uneducated" out, MHS did not require oral or written tests to enroll. Theoretically, all Hawaii high schools were open to all students. But by requiring students to take oral and written tests, those who spoke English at home gravitated toward the English Standard School, while those with difficulty with phonetics wound up at nonstandard schools, such as McKinley High School. "The result was a dual public school system, created along racial and social lines," wrote historian Theon Wright in "The Disenfranchised Islands." At the same time, teachers coming from the mainland, feeling as if they were in a foreign country, stressed the American experience. Political sociologist Lawrence Fuchs explained that teachers in public schools concentrated on American history and government, free enterprise and the meaning of democracy. "America was individualistic, full of opportunity and reward," he said. "It was, in short, everything that their homes and Hawaii were not." Historian Bob Dye called it a "program of Americanization." The result: high school students of the 1930s who attended nonstandard English public schools were taught to believe in the promises of America.

I Know Your Name

Swastika?
Yes.
Am I pronouncing your name correctly?
Yes.

Your last name is foreign
to you and others,
truncated or misspelled.
My father said
our last name had *other* letters.

J and B were sure
they had discovered my name.
"Hi SHUR-leee," they exclaimed one day
while Mrs. H and I were in the process
of packing to move classrooms (again).
"We know your real name," they smiled.
"We read it on a box.
We know who you are."

Is It Okay If We Call You

"Are you mad we found out?" J asked.
"Are you surprised we're so smart?" B smiled.
"We can call you Shirley now?" J asked.
"You can call me Boy," B offered.
"What's wrong with your real name?"
"That's what teachers call me."

S and K

"K, you speak full on Japanese?"
"I can. I was born there."
"It was OK. I was teased a lot."
"For being kuroi."
"I like Hawaii better."
"Everyone thinks I'm Filipino."
"Do you think I look Japanese?"
"Sometimes I wonder what if—"
"Yeah, Tonga or Sāmoa."
"When we visit it's fun. Same with Japan."
"I wish!"
"Huh?"
"I dunno. Ask Miss Shirley."
"Our teacher."
"It is."
"It's her real name."
"Yes, Jun said."
"Jun. JUN. You know him. Dionisio."
"He said it was. He knows."
"Let me see."
"Representatives."
"Like Barack Obama represents us."

Real Lives

It's the last period of the day
on the last day of school.
The heat is an oven, and we are Thanksgiving ducks.
We retreat to the shade
of the Chinese banyans.
We chat on the benches about
who's going off to basic and where,
who got scholarships to play at a CC in CA,
who's a father, who's prego, who's using,
who's having domestics,
who's mad at who,
and who's causing all the dramaz.

S asks if I will come back next year.
"No," I reply, "I have another job."
"Will we still know you?"
"Of course. I'll visit."
"No," he shakes his head,
"You don't understand.
I mean will you be in our real lives
outside of school?"

Image courtesy of *Star Bulletin*, June 16, 1942

Winning Poster Artist:
Here is Edward P.S. Loo, 21, member of the Hawaii Territorial Guard, with the
poster which he prepared and which will be used in advertising the forthcoming
United National Review, army benefit show. His poster won first prize in a recent
contest. Mr. Loo graduated from McKinley High School in 1938 and since then
has been specializing in advertising, display posters, and artwork.

young man
handsome
crooked hat (military)
crooked smile
khaki backpack and slacks
small shadow
cement background
poster says
        UNITED
        NATIONS
                REVUE
        ARMY BENEFIT SHOV (W covered by fingers)

(Poster image)   bald eagle
                    stars
                    rays coming from admission price
                    like a japanese sun
June 20th to
July 5th
Show
Time (indecipherable)

Admission $1.00

INTERNATIONAL SHOW
by the Civilian Defense Recreation Committee

Lawa

S is sitting on a desk when I walk into the classroom.
Mr. X yells at him from the hallway to
"get the F off the furniture."

When X leaves, S sits back on the desk.
He lies down and kicks off his shoes.
The bell rings.
Mrs. H ignores S and begins the lesson
with the other five students who are sitting in their seats.
One of them tells S to get his A off the table.
Mrs. H shushes the student and continues the lesson.
They are learning about volcanoes.

Mrs. H writes *vulcanoes* and *lawa* on the board.
Mrs. H hands out two worksheets.
Mrs. H sits at her desk.
She tells me her brother has cancer;
his prognosis is not so good.
She says she saw two girls kissing
in the courtyard and it gave her
the heebie jeebies.
She says she can't wait
to do her three years and get out of SPED.
She says her boyfriend just lost
his job at the shipping yard and
she's going to leave him, but
after he gets back on his feet.
Mrs. H asks me if I will watch
the class when she goes to the restroom.
I know she won't be back
for a good half hour—it's become
this unspoken routine.

S finally sits down, but on the floor.
He looks up at me as I am marking papers:
"Is there any way we can get Miss H fired?"
I ask him what he thinks of the rain.
S says today he's still not gonna do his work

no matter what I say
because he knows what tactics
I'm using to redirect him and
gain his trust. He says nothing
I do will work on him
because I can't make him do anything
he doesn't want to do.

The wind blows
worksheets on the floor.
I ask him to close the window
and he does. He picks up
the worksheets and throws
them in the trash.
He picks a scab on his arm.
He says he slept at the mortuary
last night to keep
his sister company while
she worked. It was really cold, he says.

Rolling My R's

B takes refuge
in my shared classroom
during recess to play computer games,
to tell funny stories,
to ask: "Do I look fat?"
"Am I too tan?"
"Do you like dis shirt?"
"Am I too skinny?"

B speaks Tagalog and Ilokano,
and another dialect I can't pronounce properly
plus standard English and Pidgin.
He says he's learning Japanese.

He thinks it's funny how I can't roll my r's.
"Miss Shirley," he laughs,
"Just breathe out and try relax your mouth.
Try! Just try.
Don't be embarruss, I not goin laugh."

I give up saying, "I can't. It's too hard."
B frowns, and says
he doesn't think I'm really *trying*.
"Just apply yourself," he says.

Inclusion

Just do it.

L said V called him a racist.

V claimed L said he didn't want to sit next to any white people.

L then stated V was not white, but Hawaiian.

V argued she was half white.

"But you don't look white," L said, "And besides," he added, "I didn't mean *you*."

V frowned. "So," she shrugged.

L protested, "Well, I don't complain when C calls me a filthy Korean."

"But you *are* filthy," V said. "And aren't you Korean?"

"Yeah," L admitted, "I am perverted."

For the rest of their lunch period, they discussed
how V thought L looked more Vietnamese than Korean,
and how L thought V *really* didn't look white.

A throws down his book. "Mrs. H, this is like so gay. Why are you making us do this? We've done this, like, three times this week. Can't we do something, like, fun, like watch a movie?"

"Why don't you just say I don't like this?" Mrs. H answers.

"Because it *is* gay!" A answers.

"Yeah, Mrs. H, this *is* kinda gay," P says.

S throws up his hands, "See, P *is* gay and even she agrees this is *gay!*"

Mrs. H smiles. "Well, A, it's okay for P. Do you understand?"

"So it's like how you don't like us to call each other niggas around E or Mr. J?"

"What did you call me?" D asks, taking his leg down from the table.

D looked up, startled. "Nothing."

"Oh, really? Because I thought you called me a *homo*."

D turned to the boy sitting next to him, M for back up, half nervous, half laughing. "I never."

"I not mad. I just like *know* what you said. And if you goin say someting, say um to my face."

"D, apologize if you said it," I say to D.

"He didn't say that word," M explained. "He said 'D's my homie.'"

"That's right. He's my lover," D said with a high-pitched voice as he fluttered his eyelids.

D rolled his eyes, "You wish."

Mandated

During mandated reading time,
A asks, "Miss Shirley, why are they selling babies
in the newspaper? Isn't that wrong?
How can they ship babies to Hawai'i?
Won't they die? Look, it says right here,
'Help buy something these babies.
Please send money.'
That's kinda messed up, yeah, why not on TV?"

I read the advertisement.
It's for children born with cleft lips
in Cambodia, Viet Nam, Laos, and Thailand.
I explain the ad wants people to buy an operation
for the baby.

A looks upset.
He says, "Who's going help the babies?
No one reads newspapers!"

In A Book

"Did you know there used to be fishponds here?"

"Not. What kinda fish?"

"I'm not sure, but they had duck ponds, too and then rice fields."

"Miss, I'm not in a gang for play around. It's for family; cuz my dad no stay. You wen hear? He went back in again."

The lava or the developer. An end by fire; a death by growth. A clean nothingness or an overabundance. A beginning by sacrifice, expansion into the sea. A grand opening, a sea of expansion.

A says when his dad gets out they'll go fishing. He says he likes carrying the catch home and watching his dad scale the fish.

A sees the paper bag that's on my desk. He knows that I have new graffiti pens to show him and Wai. He asks me if he can borrow one for today. I tell him he can have them.

It's not gonna work he tells me. "I know you're just being nice so I'll like you and listen when you tell me for do stuff."

I don't answer.

He pauses. "Fo real?" He leans forward, presses the tips on his fingernails, allows ink to indigo his half moons.

I move on to help another student. When I come back around he's working with his pocket calculator.

Milk and Blood

In this dry place, I am traumatized by the *whack* of a barrel against bare palms. B waves from the benches in front of E building.

"Eh, how you Miss? Eh, you know dey can make diamonds from peanut buttah?"

"Oh yea?"

"No fo real you know dey can. I seen um on PBS. Dey put da peanut buttah in one microwave or somting li dat, an den dey push da button, an den come out one diamond."

"B, so what do you do now since you not in ROTC?"

He shrugs. "Get into trouble."

"Like what?"

"Me and my friends, we jump people on River Street. Miss, you not going tell yea?"

"What?"

"Ha, I jus joking. You wen believe me?" He laughs. Someone drops their rifle. *Thwack!*

"Miss, I lose weight to you? Everyone tellin me I look like I doin drugs, but I not. I just no eat cause I not hungry. I mean I hungry, but nothing fo eat at home. I mean get food, but not like good food."

The ROTC marches by in perfect formation. Mrs. K walks toward me holding out a cuff of her shirt, "Shirley, do you know how to get out a blood stain?"

Before I can answer, B says, "Milk."

Mrs. K looks at him blankly. "Excuse me," she says.

"My uncle wen tell me milk good fo take out any kine blood stain. Fo real. Da whole percent kine."

"B, you mean club soda," I smile.

"No," he shakes his head. "Milk, my uncle says dat's da bes ting fo get out da stain on da carpet, yoah clothes, any kine." A rifle spins in the air and comes down into the firm grip of a cadet.

"Club soda?" I say again.

"No, milk," he shakes his head.

"I guess milk, Eleanor," I say.

Mrs. K thanks me and walks away, her heels echoing on the pavement. The wind comes from behind, flings the dead leaves around our bodies.

When Mrs. K is out of sight B asks, "How come you neva believe my uncle?"

U.S. Senator Daniel Inouye

I Still Love You[17]

Dad, I see you crossing a stream,
       filling in a marsh.

Dad, I'm sorry I neva listen
wen you tell me no fo get
da MWH tattoo.
I wen learn my lesson.

Dad, I see you in the rain,
Dad, I see you like a tombstone,
       like a lucky cat,
       like love.

Dad, I'm sorry I no like play
football, but I ain't you.

Dad, you as *chichi* and *haha,*

Dad, I still pray
that you will come home.

Dad of 1963,
       of Commerce,
       of Moʻiliʻili,
       of stars,

Dad who you goin
caucus for? Not
the Punahou grad?

Dad, I see you hiking Kokohead,
Dad mauka,
Dad makai,
Dad of myth,

Dad, I just like forget about
you, but I neva met
you.   Come home so I can
tell you I still love you.

Dad of Defense,
            of homeland,

Dad of sacrifice,
Dad, where are you?

Out of Mānoa

Mr. D looks like Santa Claus with rosier cheeks. He tells me he's an English instructor at UH Mānoa. He subs for fun, he says, to stay connected to the real people. Right now, he's subbing for Ms. H, who's out sick again. I'm correcting papers on scatter box plots when I hear Mr. D mention the word "Africa." I lift my eyes because Ms. H teaches environmental science.

Ms. H's brightest student, G, waves her arm frantically. "So like you mean da people are starving cause they not as advanced as us Americans even in Hawaii?"

Mr. D nods, "Exactly G," he beams.

J, who hardly speaks in class, lifts his head, "So why do we have starving people here?"

Mr. D pauses, "Well," he lowers his voice, "that's because those people are probably addicted to drugs and mentally ill or their family doesn't help them out or they're just lazy and don't want to work." G smiles, "Oh I get it, like my uncle he no work, he just lay around the apartment not doin nothing?"

Mr. D answers, "Yes, exactly like that."

J turns to G, "Which uncle, da one jus got back?" G nods, "Yeah."

S, on fat

"Kelly, you're getting kinda fat," S says.

Kelly lifts her shirt, exposing a small, round belly. She breathes out so it pops out emphasizing the leanness of her arms and legs. "Why? Jealous? I'm proud of my belly," she answers. "My dad said I look good. I eat plenny. We're rich. You're too skinny."

"I'm not too skinny!" S lifts his shirt and points to his stomach. "See," he says, "I get fat too!"

S, on fire

There are pleas from the students
for soap in their bathrooms
because there is a rumor
S has contracted ringworm.
Someone says they actually "saw it."

"You can *see* it!"
"You can see *it!*"
Yesterday it was covered.
But today it's exposed,
A jagged circle of flesh,
red and pink and gray.
Its borders, dry and cracked,
the beginnings of a scar.

"It's not ringworm,
Miss Shirley," S says,
"My brother caught A and me smoking.
It was bad, the smell burns."

Real History

D sees me typing. "You can help me?" he asks. "We gotta do this thing for Mr. K. Make this family tree thing? An I like the names be all straight. I can't type cuz of my broken arm. So you can type the stuffs for me?"

"Sure, what's your father's name?" Immediately I'm sorry I asked.

He shrugs, "I no care about him. He not my real father. My dad, I mean, he not married to my mom, but Healani, he take me fishing; we go water park. He's my dad. But I can put his name or what?"

"Of course."

"Oh, gotta put like what he do fo make money Mr. said."

"Okay..."

"Put construction."

"Kay, how about your grandparents on your mother's side?"

"I don't know, Margaret, I think, or something. They live in California I think. My mother has a picture of them on the TV, but they don't talk."

"What about your brothers, what are their full names, what do they do?"

He looks away, "They all have different fathers. So their last names I not too sure."

"That's fine. So what do they do for work?"

"My brothers? I don't know, but I think one of them is gonna join the army. Anden one of um works somewhere, but I forget the name."

"That's Okay. Don't worry. We'll make that up, too."

So we make up all the names and occupations. It takes a lot longer than I expect. D is not particular, but has a hard time thinking of names and jobs that are not true.

D tells me if they go back to his great-great grandparents he'd get extra credit points. "But I no like wayse your time yeah," he says.

"You want me to help you put it together?"

He shrugs. "If you want to. I just need help make it look nice you know like one girl did um."

So I sit with him. We talk about the girl's basketball game last night as we cut out the relationships and occupations. I draw a tree and he outlines it in brown marker.

"I hope Mr. K likes it," he says, "if not, well, fuck it, it's just a grade."

Referral 4

When your dad got out and took you Big Island,
did you go to Kamehameha's fishponds?
The ones the lava flow never destroy.
No? Jus stay Uncle Billy's, cruz Ali'i Drive,
hang out Hard Rock and Lulu's.

You said you were thinking of dropping
out and joining the army,
and I asked, *how,* a little too quickly.
Perhaps you thought I was referring to something else.
Now the right words, what good will they do us now?
Believe. Change. Hope.
The referral must still be written.

I didn't catch it then. The tilt in your voice.
I thought you went outside to drink water
not to cut class. If only I could place *things*
in a cardboard box. Padlock them in Public Storage.
With all them perpendicular planes you hate so much.
And lines labeled "X" and "Y."
Continuing into infinity.
(((What does that mean? What does that look like?)))
At least so you could read "chaos" with confidence.

Someone asked you if you passed the ASVAB.
You shrugged and said they wouldn't take your flat feet.

Equations

If there are those among
us who would make our way
more difficult, we must not be
disheartened, but the more earnestly
dedicate ourselves to the task upon
which we have rightly entered.

The path of progress is seldom smooth.
New things are often found
hard to do. Our fathers
found them so. We find them so.
They are inconvenient.
They cost us something.
But are we not made better
for the effort and sacrifice, and
are not those we serve
lifted up and blessed?

President McKinley, second inaugural address, 1904

Commencement

When it's time

to be trimmed

the trees know

because the big letters come out,

The crowd will cheer, "Mission Accomplished!

You graduated"

as you cross

the *sacred* oval

preserving the *traditions*

of President McKinley's treaty.

The air will be abuzz with swift haircuts

and tiny winged insects will dive

bomb our heads.

If they are lucky, they will be brushed

away by a powerful hand such as yours.

S, on teachers

"Look, my jacket is muddy," S lifts up
the back of his stained hoodie. "Will you wash it for me?"

"Will *I* wash it?"

"Yes."

"We don't have a washing machine at school."

"Please."

"You don't think it's inappropriate to ask *me* to wash your clothes?"

"Inappropriate?"

"Strange."

"You think it's weird, Miss? How come?"

"I'm *not* your mother."
"Yeah but, you're my teacher."

S, on blood

It's time for HSA testing.
A taps my shoulder with blood
on his face, on his fingers.

"I'm bleeding," he says tilting
his head back. He says this often,
at least twice a week. Last time
it was strawberry jam. I look
in his eyes. "I'm not faking blood,"
he says. His voice prickles.

S points,
"He's been very *very* sick."
He smiles, "A get his maʻi.
It's his body,
let him clean it."

S, on religion

Yesterday when S brought bibles to school,
in all of them, A wrote "Buddha = Braddah" and
"You can't spell Jesus without Buddha."
S laughed, rolled his eyes, and
handed one to me.
"Do you believe in God?" he asked.
"If you don't, that's okay,
I just need you to take one."

Catchment

Depressions in land collect
water. You can't drink it so you guzzle warm soda.
To become purified eat some discarded ramen pigeons fight over.
Think like a rat burrowed in the pink of a mama cat.
Argue over the outline of a fish on the trunk of an old Accord.

Today's exponents, beings and
mathematical ones. Arrange them in order
of greatness(est) to least.
You're already framed
by a window with only one view.
Yesterday you tried prying
it open, but they shot you
on camera doing something *illegal*.
Today (they say) you're part of
the window, part of the view.

Your body's not invisible, but
it might as well be since
no one speaks of it, but
in band-aids
Dove soaps
laundry detergents
Shiseido creams
broadcasts
jokes
fairytales
in crumbling (KPT/ivory) towers.

You try to chip away the flesh
of the wall, wade through skin
and membrane. Where
the elasticity allows,
but I'm (you're) the threshold.
Writing your name
the date
the Period
the problems

your calculations
your answers
neatly with pencils that state my name
in permanent marker in all CAPS.
I have one less each day. My am changes
as you scratch off one more letter.
Take a walk
where π meets the sky
to the nursery on Pensacola.
See there?
The broken gutters.
The rust, the peeling paint.
See here, they sell this
ti leaf at craft fairs.
The rain drops are singing
your new alma mater, "Catch me if you can."

Oceanic Performance

Christmas Pageantry.

Background. Drama. Shakespeare.
Costumed bodies. Wiggling trees.

Foreground. Orchestra. Brass. Wind. Percussion. String.

On the ground.
Special choral performance:
1 pianist. 1 rapper. 4 back-up singers.

Please welcome, the Poly Soljahs!

> A pounds
> the table, it shakes, and
> he yells, "Polynesians for life!"
> He's not Polynesian. But neither are all of the Poly Soljahs.

> *This song is for all the people whoever lost somebody.*

Their voices are drowned
out by the brass warm-ups.

S and A hold hands. Cuz. Just cuz.

We give Poly Soljahs a standing ovation.

A wipes his glasses or something
from his eyes, maybe tears.

Chaminade / Saint Louis Bus Stop

It's summer
and the sun, rubbed out
by vog, has faded.
As I near the bus stop, I see a former student.
"Oh my god, Miss! Hurry!" he screams,
jumping up and down as the bus pulls up.
"How are you? What are you doing here?"
"I'm Angel. I got the part! I'm ANGEL!"
"That's wonderful."
"You know he's a gay guy, right? I'm playing a gay guy."
"I'm so proud of you."
"Aren't you coming," he asks.
"I live here."
"Oh yeah!"
"I'll come and see it when it opens."
"Yeah, of course you will."
"I will."
The bus driver waves
him on and closes the doors.

I stop at the bridge and look over the side
at the Pālolo Stream. It's got
debris and trash and ducks.
I watch the ducks swim
in circles, diving into the brown water.
I wonder what in this water
sustains them. Some schoolboys walk past.
"We missed it," the young one says.
"Fuck!" the tallest one yells.
"I'll call my dad to come get us," replies the other.

Warriors

One night on my way home from the airport, the bus I'm riding breaks down in Chinatown. I've just gotten back from Kona where I visited my mom in the hospital. I get off, dragging my suitcase, and right away I hear this voice. One of my students.

"Eh, Miss," he yells from across the street, "how you?" He sees my luggage. "My uncle, he drive cab," he says. And then he calls him.

I ask how he's doing. He says he's sorry he hasn't been coming to class, but he's been taking care of his little cousin who's sick and no one else can stay home and watch him. He says he wants to graduate this year, but now his mom guys are telling him he might as well quit school for now and get a job like his uncles. He says he's thinking about it because his uncles work construction and then at night drive cab. He says they make good money and sometimes they still get time for kick back, chillax, and drink beers. But he's not sure cuz his sister told him don't do it.

Then he asks me how I am doing. I bring up the weather, how it's been too hot, and ask him if he thinks the Warriors are good enough to beat Washington. He nods, says we're probably make it all the way to a bowl game if we're lucky. He points to the sky, it's global warming he says about the heat.

His uncle comes before the next bus. His uncle is friendly and asks me if I was born here. In the cab, we chit chat about the heat, how it's been so humid and voggy, and if the Warriors are gonna beat Washington on Saturday.

The McKinley girls basketball team won the league championship twice, first in 1911, then in 1916. Left to right, front row—Molly Thompson, Thelma Wicke, Elizabeth Fuller. Second row—Lucy Holt, Rosalie Holt, Helen Duncan. Back row—Mary Prestige, Hattie Pauole.

Endnotes

[1] Italics and line breaks are my own. Quote from *Sites of Oahu.*

[2] Fox News reported the rainfall as a "near biblical downpour." http://www.foxnews.com/story/0,2933,190218,00.html

[3] From *A Hundred Years: McKinley High School 1865-1965.* Foreword by Principal Teichiro Hirata.

[4] McKinley's alma mater: "Hail, McKinley, hail,/ Hail, McKinley, hail,/ Thy sons and daughters sing thy praise, / And loyal serve thee all their days. / Alma Mater, thee alone we love / And thy colors floating high above. / Hail, McKinley, hail, / All hail, all hail."

[5] McKinley HS was considered a feeder school to Princeton in the 60s.

[6] *Lost* shot a flashback scene with actress Michelle Rodriguez as a police officer in LA. The scene included driving down King Street and McKinley HS was clearly visible in the background.

[7] Fort Street English Day School (FSEDS) was started in 1865 by Reverend Maurice Beckwith in the basement of the Old Fort Street Church. FSEDS eventually became McKinley High School.

[8] The date of President McKinley's statue dedication to MHS in Honolulu.

[9] President McKinley was assassinated by a gun, which was concealed under a handkerchief.

[10] Historical information taken from a secondary social studies book used in public schools.

[11] From Nina Wu's article in the Star Bulletin, "Kakaako rich with Hawaiian history." I have change the order of her information and the order of some of the words in her article. Bryan Kuwada, one of our editors, disagrees with some of Wu's reporting, namely that Kewalo and Kakaʻako are the same area. Here is a part of the article with some parts removed. Wu interviewed Lurline Naone-Salvador. From her consulting company, Kahiliʻula Associates, Naone-Salvador, "researches and recommends appropriate Hawaiian names to developers for their projects." It is unclear in the article whether Wu finds this information on Kakaʻako / Kewalo by her own research or if she is summarizing something Naone-Salvador has said. I have included the information I found here in this collection for the reader to decipher.

[12] Diacritical is used in the article, however, it is the newspaper's own diacritical mark.

[13] Brill, Richard. Business column: Facts of the Matter. "Stream Seek Equilibrium but Never Find It." Honolulu Star Bulletin. 15 Mar 2005.

[14] Inspired by a conversation with two students.

[15] From William Carlos Williams: "In the end the man rises from the sea where the river appears to have lost its identity."

[16] Star Bulletin. "Boom Under the Hula Moon." I modified some of the language, but the meat of the article remains.

[17] Format from and some wording from a poem in a Hawaiian newspaper. (See Beckwith, *Hawaiian Mythology*, 30). My poem was inspired by Senator Daniel Inouye, who graduated from McKinley High School. In fact, at times, he has used this as a divisive point. Recall his comments about Barack Obama going to Punahou, which is a prestigious private institution in Honolulu.

About the Author

Jill Yamasawa was born in Kona, Hawaii and raised in Holualoa and Honaunau on citrus and coffee farms. Her paternal great-grandparents were from Hiroshima, but the ancestry of her maternal great-grandparents is unknown. She graduated from Konawaena High School. She has a BA in American and British Literature from Santa Clara University and an MA in creative writing from the University of Hawai'i at Mānoa where she also studied fine arts. She teaches writing at Roosevelt High School. Jill has been published in *Paradigm* (2007), *Ka Lamakua* (2008), *HOW2* (2008) and *Tinfish* (2008). This is her first book of poems.

www.ingramcontent.com/pod-product-compliance
Lightning Source LLC
Chambersburg PA
CBHW062013040426
42447CB00010B/2018